Avoid climbing Mount Everest!

Written by
Ian Graham

Illustrated by
David Antram

Created and designed by
David Salariya

The Danger Zone™

BOOK HOUSE

Contents

Introduction   5

Mount Everest   6

Into the death zone   8

Picking the team   10

Testing times   12

Nepal   14

Base camp   16

Moving supplies   18

The plan for the top   20

The Mallory mystery   22

The first attempt   24

The back-up plan   26

On top of the world   28

Glossary   30

Index   32

Author:
Ian Graham studied applied physics at the City
University, London. He then took a postgraduate
degree in journalism, specialising in science and
technology. Since becoming a freelance author and
journalist, he has written more than one hundred
children's non-fiction books.

Artist:
David Antram was born in Brighton, England,
in 1958. He studied at Eastbourne College of Art
and then worked in advertising for fifteen years
before becoming a full-time artist. He has
illustrated many children's non-fiction books.

Series creator:
David Salariya was born in Dundee, Scotland.
He has illustrated a wide range of books and has
created and designed many new series for
publishers in the UK and overseas. David
established The Salariya Book Company in 1989.
He lives in Brighton, England, with his wife,
illustrator Shirley Willis, and their son Jonathan.

Editor: **Jamie Pitman**

Editorial Assistant: **Mark Williams**

Published in Great Britain in MMX by
Book House, an imprint of
The Salariya Book Company Ltd
25 Marlborough Place, Brighton BN1 1UB
www.salariya.com
www.book-house.co.uk

HB ISBN-13: 978-1-906714-31-4
PB ISBN-13: 978-1-906714-32-1

SALARIYA

1 3 5 7 9 8 6 4 2

A CIP catalogue record for this book is available
from the British Library.

Printed and bound in Singapore.

Visit our website at **www.book-house.co.uk**
or go to **www.salariya.com** for **free** electronic versions of:
You Wouldn't Want to be an Egyptian Mummy!
You Wouldn't Want to be a Roman Gladiator!
You Wouldn't Want to be a Polar Explorer!
You Wouldn't Want to sail on a 19th-Century Whaling Ship!

PAPER FROM
SUSTAINABLE
FORESTS

Introduction

The year is 1952 and you are a keen climber. When you're not at work, you head for the mountains. You've climbed mountains all over Britain, and the Alps, a mountain range in western Europe. A peak called Mount Everest in the Himalayas is especially interesting to mountaineers everywhere. It is the world's tallest mountain, but no-one has managed to climb to the top of it yet. A team of Swiss climbers is on Mount Everest right now. You hear rumours that if the Swiss expedition fails, a British team will be the next to try. It would be great to climb Mount Everest, but you can only do it by being a member of an official expedition – and you can only join an expedition if you are invited. You dream of getting a chance to join an Everest expedition.

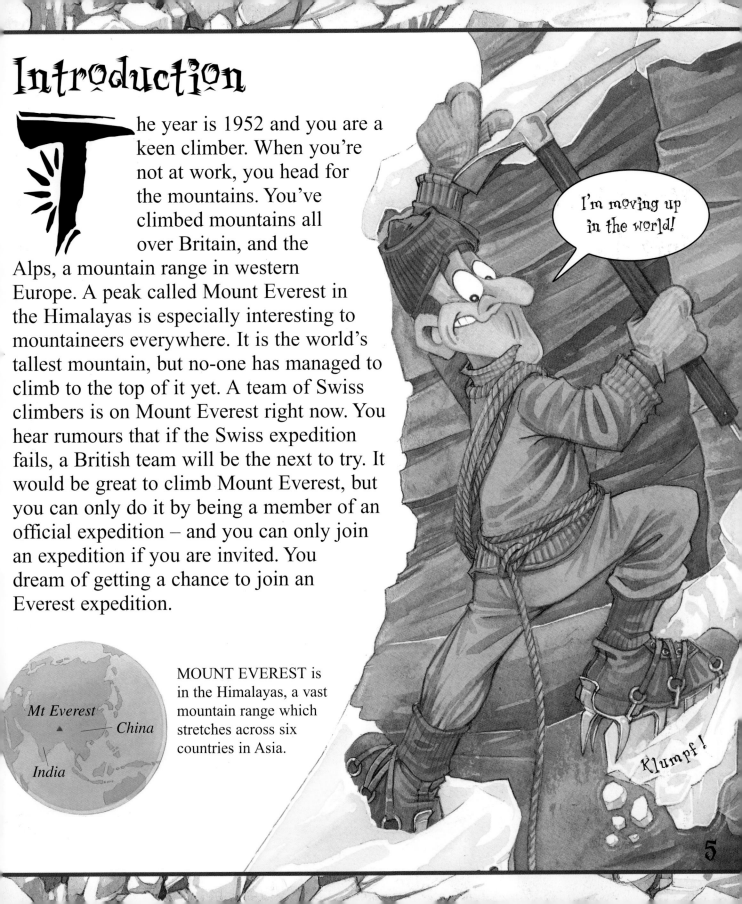

I'm moving up in the world!

Klumpf!

Mt Everest
China
India

MOUNT EVEREST is in the Himalayas, a vast mountain range which stretches across six countries in Asia.

Mount Everest

Summit

South summit
A dome of rock just below Mt Everest's summit

Everest

Everest is the world's tallest mountain. It stands 8,850 metres high. It was named by the British after Colonel Sir George Everest. He had been the Surveyor General of India at a time when India was ruled by Great Britain. His job was to survey India so that accurate maps could be drawn. Local people know Everest by different names. In Nepal it is called Sagarmatha, meaning 'Goddess of the sky'. In Tibet it is Qomolangma Feng, meaning 'Mother of the Universe'. When people learned that it was the world's tallest mountain, the race was on to climb it.

Sir George Everest

Colonel Sir George Everest (1790–1866) spent more than 25 years surveying India. It is not known whether he ever saw the great mountain that was named after him.

FLAG CLOUD. A white triangular cloud called the 'flag cloud' appears on the east side of Mount Everest in winter and spring. Its shape tells climbers how fast the wind is blowing at the summit.

South col
A gap between Mt Everest and Lhotse

Lhotse

Nuptse

Handy hint

Check your ropes and knots – your life may depend on them.

Lhotse face
One side of Lhotse, the fourth highest mountain on Earth

Western cwm
A valley carved out by a glacier

Khumbu Icefall
Part of the Khumbu glacier

Theodolite

THEODOLITES. Measurements of angles for the Survey of India were made using instruments called theodolites. Each weighed more than half a tonne and needed 12 men to carry it.

Into the death zone

I f you climb Mount Everest, you risk being buried by snowfalls or falling down deep cracks in the ice called crevasses. Higher up the mountain, more dangers await you. The air is so thin that just walking a few steps makes you gasp for breath. At the summit, it can be so cold that bare skin freezes in seconds! It is so dangerous above about 7,300 metres that climbers call this region the 'death zone'. You can only survive at this altitude for two or three days.

IF YOU HEAR a rumbling sound, run! It could be an avalanche – a torrent of snow and ice sliding down the mountainside.

Rumble! Rumble!

Shiver!

THE TEMPERATURE at the top of Mount Everest averages –36°C, but it can fall as low as –60°C.

How long am I going to have to hang around here for?

Hold on a minute!

Slip!

Whoosh!

CRAMPONS. Above about 5,000 metres in the Himalayas, ice and snow cover the ground all year round. Climbers wear sets of spikes called 'crampons' on their boots. The spikes stick into the ice. Don't forget to put them on or you'll slip and fall!

AVOID CLIMBING Mount Everest between June and September and between November and March. During these periods the weather is at its worst. You'll be hit by storms, heavy snowfall, thick clouds, hurricane-strength winds and avalanches.

Picking the team

John Hunt, a British army officer, is to lead the expedition to Mount Everest in 1953. His first job is to choose his team of climbers. He draws up a list of experienced mountaineers aged 25 to 40. You are delighted when you receive a letter inviting you to join the expedition as part of a team of ten climbers. In addition, there will be an expedition doctor, a physiologist and a film cameraman. They are all from Britain and Commonwealth countries (the Commonwealth is a group of countries that were once part of the British Empire). Later, one more person will be invited to join the climbing team, bringing the total to 14.

THE JOINT HIMALAYAN COMMITTEE organises British attempts on Mount Everest. John Hunt is selected to head the 1953 expedition because he is a good all-round mountaineer with military leadership experience.

EDMUND HILLARY is a bee-keeper from New Zealand. An experienced climber, he took part in an Everest expedition in 1951.

TOM STOBART will make a film of the expedition, because there is already a lot of public interest.

MICHAEL WARD is the expedition's doctor. He is also a good climber, so he will join the climbing team if anyone drops out.

Testing times

I n December 1952, you go to Switzerland with John Hunt and two other climbers to test clothing and equipment. You take eight types of boots and try a different pair each day. The four of you swap clothes and compare notes on which is the best. You test tents by trying to put them up in a blizzard. The day before you come home, you hear that the Swiss team has failed to reach the summit of Everest. The British attempt is on!

GLOVES. The climbers will wear three-part gloves. The first layer is a loose-fitting silk glove, which is covered with the second layer, a woollen mitt. Finally, a windproof cotton gauntlet forms the outer layer.

BOOTS. Two types of boots are made for the expedition. One is a light boot for the first part of the climb. The other has extra insulation for colder conditions.

What's the verdict, then?

NEAR THE TOP of Mount Everest, the climbers will wear oxygen equipment to help them breathe more easily. You try it out on your return from Switzerland in January. You wear a set of oxygen cylinders on your back and breathe through a pilot's face mask.

Lightweight metal cylinders

Economiser reduces oxygen waste

Valves control pressure and flow

Handy hint

Keep every part of your body covered or you'll get frostbite.

Whoosh!

It's a great kite, but a lousy tent!

Skreee!

MOST OF THE EXPEDITION'S TENTS are two-man ridge tents. Three smaller tents will be used for the highest camps. In addition, two big 12-man tents will be used at the main camps.

Nepal

The climbers arrive at Kathmandu in Nepal by sea and air, along with 473 packing cases full of supplies weighing 7.6 tonnes. The supplies will have to be carried on foot from Kathmandu to Mount Everest by 350 porters and 36 Sherpas. The walk will take 16 days. Sherpas are a people from the foothills of Mount Everest. They are very skilled climbers.

I wonder if we packed enough fruit cake.

The Sherpas will carry the supplies to camps higher up the mountain. Their leader, or *sirdar*, for this expedition is Tenzing Norgay. He is 38 years old and this will be the sixth time he has climbed Everest. He has worked on almost every Everest expedition since 1935 and nearly reached the summit with the unsuccessful Swiss expedition.

Handy hint

Don't wear brand-new boots – you'll get blisters.

WHEN THE SHERPAS arrive, they line up for inspection wearing a variety of clothes collected from earlier expeditions. There are ski hats, balaclavas, berets and brightly coloured jumpers.

TENZING NORGAY is asked to join the climbing party because of his great experience and climbing ability. He has more experience on Everest than any other Sherpa, having climbed to within 300 metres of the great mountain's summit.

ALL THE SUPPLIES are divided up between the porters and Sherpas. The packs are weighed to make sure they are not too heavy to carry. The standard weight for each person is about 27 kilograms.

Base camp

O n 10 March, everyone sets off from Kathmandu to Thyangboche at the foot of Mount Everest. Twelve porters are needed to carry the porters' wages, because they will only accept payment in coins, not paper money. Each day, you have to start walking soon after 6.00 a.m. The kitchen staff go ahead and find somewhere to prepare the next meal. The base camp is set up near a Buddhist monastery. The climbers train for three weeks to get used to the altitude.

Say 'aah'...

Pant!

TRADITIONAL HEAD STRAPS are used by the porters to carry large loads.

WHEN THE TEAM ARRIVES, local people quickly queue up to visit its doctor, Michael Ward. He pulls patients' rotten teeth and treats lots of minor illnesses.

GRIFFITH PUGH, the physiologist, gives you a 'maximum work test'. He times you while you run uphill until your lungs feel like they are bursting.

'Abominable?' What cheek!

THE PORTERS are paid for their hard work. The same day, they begin the long walk back to their villages across Nepal.

THE MONKS are full of stories about the Yeti, or Abominable Snowman, a human-like creature thought by some to live in Nepal and Tibet.

Moving supplies

Climbers and Sherpas are always climbing up and down the mountain, moving supplies to camps higher up. They have to go through one of the most dangerous parts of the climb – the icefall. It's a treacherous part of the Khumbu glacier, a constantly moving river of ice. The cracked ice has split into huge blocks with deep crevasses between them. It makes loud cracks as it moves. Every morning, the ice has moved so much that a new route has to be found through it. Crevasses that could be stepped across one day are so wide the next day that they can only be crossed by using bridges.

THE ICEFALL is so difficult and dangerous to cross that bridges and ladders have to be used in some places. They have to be strong enough to hold the weight of a porter and the load he carries on his back.

After this, I'm definitely going to 'ave-a-rest'!

Let's hope the Icefall doesn't live up to its name!

Handy hint

Don't forget to use your ice axe to test the snow for hidden crevasses before you step on it.

CRAMPONS are essential for climbing on ice. The metal spikes stick into the ice and stop the boots from slipping.

SUNLIGHT reflected by snow and ice is so bright that you have to wear dark glasses called snow goggles. Some of the Sherpas have made their own snow goggles from cardboard and cellophane.

19

The plan for the top

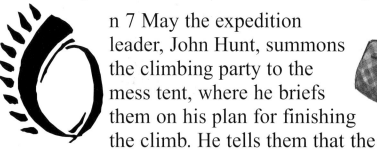

On 7 May the expedition leader, John Hunt, summons the climbing party to the mess tent, where he briefs them on his plan for finishing the climb. He tells them that the first attempt on the summit will be made by Tom Bourdillon and Charles Evans. The two climbers will aim to reach the south summit, a dome of rock just below the top of the mountain. Once there, they will decide whether they can carry on to the top. If they can't, Tenzing and Hillary will make a second attempt straight away. After the briefing, everyone settles back into their daily routine.

The daily routine

DAYTIME ACTIVITIES are planned around meal times. It's so cold that you stay in your sleeping bag when you're not training.

YOUR BREATH freezes on the inside of the tent during the night. Sometimes you are woken by ice falling on you as the morning sun warms the tent.

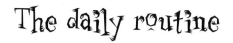

A SHERPA brings you a mug of steaming hot tea first thing in the morning.

Wakey wakey!

BREAKFAST is ready at 8.45 a.m. – a bowl of porridge followed by bacon and eggs or fried luncheon meat.

Slurp!

So this is it!

Handy hint

Don't forget to wear your goggles or you'll get snow blindness.

LUNCH is at midday. You have soup with salami sausage and cheese, washed down with coffee.

Munch!

IT'S TIME FOR TEA at 4.00 p.m. You have tea, biscuits, and maybe some fruit cake.

SUPPER is served at sundown. You have soup and tinned steak and kidney pie, followed by coffee and fruit cake.

BETWEEN MEALS, you write letters home. It's so cold that the ink in your pen freezes.

The Mallory mystery

s the climbers prepare for the final assault on Mount Everest's summit, they wonder if they might find signs that someone has beaten them to it. During an expedition in 1924, British climbers George Mallory and Sandy Irvine were spotted on their way to the summit. They never returned and no-one knows whether they got to the top. Since 1921, about 175 climbers and Sherpas have died on the mountain. Many of their bodies are still there to this day, because it's far too dangerous to carry them down.

THE CLOTHING worn by mountaineers in the 1920s was very simple. Mallory's team wore many layers of thin silk, cotton, and wool to protect them against the cold. Here they are wearing street clothes at Base Camp.

Handy hint

Don't touch anything outside with your bare skin or you'll be frozen to it in an instant.

MALLORY was one of the most experienced climbers of his day. He took part in all three British expeditions to Mount Everest in the 1920s.

IRVINE was very good at repairing things, especially oxygen equipment.

IN 1999, MALLORY'S BODY was found on a rocky slope at a height of about 8,170 metres. The items found with his body included his snow goggles, a tin of sweets, an altimeter and a watch. No camera was found, so we still don't know whether he reached the summit.

The first attempt

On 26 May, Tom Bourdillon and Charles Evans set out from Camp 8 at 7,925 metres. Later that day, they become the first climbers ever to reach the south summit at over 8,748 metres.

Tired and running low on oxygen, they realise that there isn't enough daylight for them to get to the summit and back to Camp 8 before nightfall. They desperately want to reach the summit, but they know if they go on it could cost them their lives. They turn back. On the way down, Evans slips. He hurtles down the slope, sweeping Bourdillon off his feet too. Incredibly, Bourdillon manages to jab his ice axe into the snow and save them both.

Must... hold... on!

Tumble!

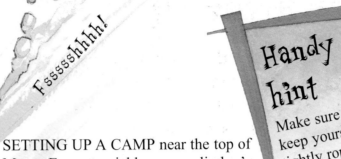

Handy hint

Make sure you keep yourself tightly roped to another climber.

Fsssssshhh!

SETTING UP A CAMP near the top of Mount Everest quickly saps a climber's strength. A task that takes a few minutes at sea level takes over an hour in the thin, freezing air at high altitude.

Woosh!

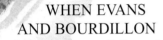

WHEN EVANS AND BOURDILLON get back to Camp 8 from the south summit, they are totally exhausted. They have to rest for some time before they begin to recover.

AS YOU MOVE supplies up the mountain, you discover an abandoned Swiss camp. You look for useful equipment and find tins of sardines (above). Tasty!

THE TEAM LEADER at the Advanced Base Camp keeps in touch with climbers higher up the mountain by radio (right).

The back-up plan

Hillary and Tenzing have already been moving up the mountain from the Advanced Base Camp, just in case the first attempt on the summit fails. Now it's their turn. Each of them carries a set of oxygen cylinders plus an 18-kilogram pack of supplies on his back. Just walking in these conditions while carrying such a heavy load takes a huge effort. They set up Camp 9 at 8,504 metres. After a meal, they settle down for the night. The temperature is –27°C. The sub-zero temperatures and the wind battering their tent make it almost impossible to sleep. After a restless night, they are tired and cold, but cheered by the thought that they are now within striking distance of the summit.

HILLARY AND TENZING pause for breath at 8,321 metres before moving supplies up to Camp 9.

AT CAMP 9, they make coffee and eat tinned apricots. They have to thaw the frozen apricots on their stove.

OXYGEN. They have so little oxygen left that they can allow themselves only four hours' supply for sleeping.

BACK AT THE ADVANCED BASE CAMP, you look up at the mountain and wonder if Hillary and Tenzing have survived the night.

On top of the world

Flag of the United Nations

Flag of Great Britain

Flag of Nepal

Flag of India

At 6.30 a.m. on 29 May 1953, Tenzing and Hillary crawl out of their tent. They cross the last ridge and climb a huge block of rock that will become known as the Hillary Step, because at 11.30 a.m. Hillary steps onto the summit with Tenzing just a pace behind. They agree to say that they reached the summit together. Tenzing, a Buddhist, buries some chocolate and biscuits in the snow as an offering to the gods. Hillary leaves a crucifix given to him by Hunt and takes a photograph of Tenzing on the summit. After 15 minutes, they begin the long journey down.

HILLARY'S BOOTS are frozen solid in the morning. He has to heat them on the stove to thaw them out before he can put them on. Tenzing keeps his warm by wearing them all night.

Pong!

Handy hint

Don't forget to take a camera with you to prove how high you were able to climb.

YOU ARE THRILLED when Hillary and Tenzing return safely with news of their success. There are handshakes and hugs all round.

It's not the mountain we conquer, but ourselves.

THE CLIMBERS arrive at London Airport on 3 July. Their success on Everest is headline news all over the world. Hillary and Tenzing are famous.

HILLARY AND HUNT were awarded knighthoods and Tenzing the George Medal by the newly crowned Queen Elizabeth II. Later, Hillary was appointed New Zealand's High Commissioner to India. Tenzing became the first director of field training at the Himalayan Mountaineering Institute. Tenzing Norgay GM died in 1986 and Sir Edmund Hillary passed away in 2008.

Glossary

Advanced Base Camp Also known as ABC; the camp set up at the base of the Lhotse face.

Altimeter An instrument which measures altitude.

Altitude Height above sea level.

Avalanche A big fall of snow and ice down a mountainside.

Blizzard A storm with strong winds and heavy snow.

British Empire A group of countries and territories that were once governed by the United Kingdom.

Buddhist A member of a religion with its roots in ancient India.

Col A mountain pass; a way through a chain of mountains.

Commonwealth A group of countries, most of which were once part of the British Empire.

Crampons Metal spikes fitted to climbing boots to give a climber better grip on ice.

Crevasse A deep crack in a glacier.

Cwm A hollow or valley on the side of a mountain.

Death zone The part of any mountain above about 7,000 metres, where there is too little oxygen in the air to support human life for more than a few days.

Expedition A journey organised to acheive a particular objective.

Frostbite Damage to flesh caused by extreme cold.

Gauntlet A protective outer glove.

George Medal An award for great courage, given to a United Kingdom or Commonwealth civilian.

Glacier A river of ice moving slowly down a slope.

Himalayas A mountain range more than 2,400 km long, extending through six countries, including northern India, Nepal and Bhutan.

Icefall A steep sheet of ice in a glacier, often looking like a frozen waterfall.

Knighthood An honour given by the British monarch to a man for a great achievement, making him a knight and giving him the title 'Sir'.

Maximum work test A test to learn how much work someone can do before becoming exhausted.

Mess tent A tent where meals are eaten.

Mitt A glove with one section for all four fingers and another for the thumb.

Physiologist A scientist who studies the functions and activities of living organisms.

Porter A person employed to carry baggage.

Ridge tent A tent with a pole along the middle of the roof, forming a ridge.

Sherpa A member of a Himalayan people living in Nepal and Tibet, famous for their mountaineering skill.

Snow blindness A painful eye condition caused by looking at bright sunlight reflected by snow and ice.

Snow goggles Dark glasses worn to prevent snow blindness.

Summit The highest point; the top of a mountain.

Survey To make an accurate plan of the ground using special surveying equipment.

Theodolite An instrument used by surveyors for measuring angles very accurately.

Yeti The Abominable Snowman, a legendary human-like creature that some people believe lives in the Himalayas.

Index

A

Abominable Snowman 17
Advanced Base Camp 25, 26
avalanche 8, 9

B

base camp 14, 16
boots 12, 15, 19, 28
Bourdillon, Tom 20, 24, 25
Buddhists 16, 28

C

cameraman 10
clothes 12, 22
Commonwealth 10
crampons 9, 19
crevasse 8, 18, 19

D

death zone 8, 9
doctor 10, 16

E

Evans, Charles 20, 24, 25
Everest, Colonel Sir George 6

F

flag cloud 6
food 16, 20, 21
frostbite 13

G

gloves 12

H

Hillary, Sir Edmund 10, 20, 26,
   28, 29
Hillary Step 28
Himalayan Mountaineering
   Institute 29
Himalayas 6
Hunt, John 10, 12, 20, 29

I

ice axe 19
icefall 7, 18
Irvine, Sandy 22, 23

J

Joint Himalayan Committee 10

K

Kathmandu 14
Khumbu glacier 18

M

Mallory, George 22, 23
maximum work test 16
meals 20, 21

N

Nepal 6

O

oxygen equipment 13, 15, 26

P

payment 16
physiologist 10, 16
porters 14, 15, 16, 17, 18
Pugh, Griffith 16

Q

Qomolangma Feng 6

R

radio 25

S

Sagarmatha 6
Sherpas 14, 18, 19, 20, 22
snow goggles 19, 21, 23
south summit 20, 24, 25
Stobart, Tom 10

T

tents 12, 13, 26, 28
Tenzing Norgay 15, 20, 26, 28,
   29
theodolite 7
Thyangboche 16
Tibet 6

W

Ward, Michael 10, 14, 16

Y

Yeti 17